THE SOLID BEAT CONCEPT

*A Modern Method for
Musical Artistic Advancement*

THE SOLID BEAT CONCEPT

*A Modern Method for
Musical Artistic Advancement*

BILLY KILSON

Copyright © 2017 by Billy Kilson. All rights reserved.

No part of this publication may be reproduced, stored in a retrieval system, or transmitted in any form or by any means, electronic, mechanical, photocopying, recording, scanning, or otherwise, without the prior written permission of the author.

Limit of Liability/Disclaimer of Warranty: While the publisher and author have used their best efforts in preparing this book, they make no representations or warranties with respect to the accuracy or completeness of the contents of this book and specifically disclaim any implied warranties of merchantability or fitness for a particular purpose. No warranty may be created or extended by sales representatives or written sales materials. The advice and strategies contained herein may not be suitable for your situation. You should consult with a professional when appropriate. Neither the publisher nor the author shall be liable for any loss of profit or any other commercial damages, including but not limited to special, incidental, consequential, personal, or other damages.

The Solid Beat Concept:
A Modern Method for Musical Artistic Advancement
by Billy Kilson

1. Music/General
2. Genres & Styles/International
3. Instruction & Study/Techniques

ISBN: 978-1-935953-85-2

Cover design by Lewis Agrell

Printed in the United States of America

Authority Publishing
11230 Gold Express Dr. #310-413
Gold River, CA 95670
800-877-1097
www.AuthorityPublishing.com

Acknowledgements

To my wife and children, you're my light.
Troy & Sharmarie, you guys are simply the greatest.
To Ron Savage and Paulie,
thanks so much for your never-ending inspiration.
Also, a heartfelt thanks to DW, Sabian, Promark, Evans,
and Reunion Blues for your unending support.

"It's a great thing about being a musician;
you don't stop until the day you die,
you can improve. So it's a wonderful thing to do."

Marcus Miller

ABOUT THE AUTHOR

In the span of almost four decades, renowned GRAMMY Award®-winning drummer Billy Kilson has set a standard all his own. Constantly evolving in his craft, philosophy, and approach, Kilson hits the mark every time. As a side man with Chris Botti over the last decade, Billy has shared the stage with some of the most prolific icons of our generation: Sting, Yo-Yo Ma, Steven Tyler, and John Mayer just to name a few. With Botti, Kilson has toured the world and entertained millions with his infectious grooves, standing-ovation-worthy drum solos, and charismatic charm.

As the leader of his own group, BK Groove, Billy released three highly acclaimed albums and elevated what it means to be a drummer in the postmodern music industry. When not touring, Billy teaches at Berklee College of Music in Boston where he's passing down the timeless wisdom and knowledge handed to him by his friend and mentor, Alan Dawson.

Contents

Foreword xi
Preface xiii
Introduction 1
    Alan Dawson's Rudimental Ritual 1
    Diversity and Adaptability 2
    Creative Learning 3
    Competition 4
Chapter 1: The Solid Beat Checklist 5
    Your Playing Environment 6
    The Solid Beat Concept Checklist 6
    Developing the Three Senses 7
    Musical Style and Authenticity 8
Chapter 2: Identify the Time Signature 11
    4/4 Time 12
    3/4 Time 12
    5/4 Time 12
    Identifying the Time Signature in Complex Situations 13
Chapter 3: Predict the Feel 14
    Creating Your Mental Rolodex 14
    Rhythmic Pacing 17
    Contributing to the Music 19
    Style Drivers 20
    Practice 22
Chapter 4: Groove Pulse Rhythms 23
    Groove Pulse 1 24
    Groove Pulse 2 24
    Groove Pulse 3 24
    Groove Pulses 4, 5, and More 24
    Making Musical Choices 25
Chapter 5: Execute the Beat 28
Chapter 6: Real World Application of The Solid Beat Concept 31

Appendix A: A Student's Perspective 33
Appendix B: Billy's Favorite Drummers and Bass Player Duos 37
Appendix C: The Rudimental Ritual 39
Glossary 41
Recommended Resources for Further Reading and Studies 43
Bibliography 45

Foreword

> "Here we use the Socratic method: I call on you;
> I ask you a question; you answer it.
> Why don't I just give you a lecture?
> Because through my questions you learn to teach yourselves.
> By this method of questioning-answering, questioning-answering,
> we seek to develop in you the ability to analyze
> the vast complex of facts that constitutes the relationships
> of members within a given society."
>
> Professor Kingsfield in *The Paper Chase*

I asked for two things when Billy contacted me to help with this book. One was that I write the foreword. The other request can be seen in Appendix A.

My name is Troy Dares, and I am Billy Kilson's longest-serving student. It's funny how the last almost sixteen years have gone by. During that time, I have seen many evolutions in Billy's playing, but all have been built on the foundation of groove and musicianship.

In 2012, Billy was asked to give a clinic for the Percussive Arts Societies International Convention (PASIC). Billy reached out to me to help develop his vision for how that clinic would go. Over the next few weeks, we rehashed almost every conversation and lesson we'd had over the previous ten plus years trying to distill his vision into a forty-five minute lecture that would provide participants a simple, practical method for forming a solid beat, which is the core of what we do as drummers.

Billy's vision was clear in his mind. He wanted a simple 3x5 index card that expressed a set of tools—a checklist—to show drummers a way to build a solid beat in any style while allowing them to be authentic by keeping their individual musical voice.

At first, I thought the task was impossible. But, as Billy shared his vision, it soon became clear. The problem for me was that it was too simple. It was so simple, I thought no one would believe it. Unfortunately, due to Hurricane Sandy, the clinic was postponed until 2014. The clinic Billy gave for 2014 PASIC was a resounding success. He received a standing ovation. Half of the convention participants asked for a book while the other half tried to come to terms with the simplicity of the method.

After seeing the positive impact from the convention, I experimented with my students. Not only did it work but I had incredible breakthroughs in ways I did not think possible. I realized the problem in accepting the ideas was my cognitive bias that there must be more

Foreword

to them. The hardest part for me was coming to terms with the fact that it really could be this easy. I have been teaching this method to my students ever since with amazing results.

There is now a vast array of literature for drum and percussion methods and principles. Regrettably, that material makes it easy for new students to get lost and waste time pondering just what to do. In addition, it is easy to forget the fundamentals while pursuing advanced methods. I constantly encounter students who are focusing on high-level issues of musical methodologies, strategy, and career development, but have completely ignored creating a solid foundation at the level where the real work is done.

In this brief volume, Billy will help you find your voice by focusing on the solid beat. The material is ordered in a way that builds on itself, provides opportunities for self-discovery, and offers a tool kit for new drummers. Billy does this by using the question and answer format that will help you remove the most common barriers so you can focus on the real work.

I sincerely believe that the only way we can cement individual learning is through our deductive processes. This book, while a set of tools, does not present you with a final set of conclusions. The musical problems you face today may have a different answer tomorrow or the next day. So you must be prepared to face the unforeseeable with an open mind. At best, a set of conclusions is the way we are trained, but it is not the way we learn.

The ideas in this book are rooted in the Socratic method and, if applied with an open mind, can solve any musical question you are faced with.

The contents of this book will help give you direction should you face road blocks in your playing and groove.

Good luck and keep practicing.

Troy Dares

PREFACE

> "If you want something new,
> you have to stop doing something old."
>
> Peter Drucker

My former student and good friend Troy says my drumming style reminds him of the story of Proteus. He tells me, "Billy, you are able to adapt your drumming methods to fit most musical settings." While I'm not the biggest fan of Greek mythology, I find this old man of the sea intriguing.

Proteus was the shape-shifting, prophet subordinate of Poseidon. The word *protean*—meaning malleable, flexible, and able to assume different forms—is derived from the story of Proteus and serves as a model for what it takes to be a successful musician.

I started out as a wannabe go-go drummer and eventually shaped myself into a jazz drummer. Through that shift, and no matter the style, one thing stayed consistent: playing a good, solid beat.

I've had the good fortune of performing with Hank Jones, Ahmad Jamal, Sting, George Duke, Bob James, and the list goes on. But no matter the style—from traditional jazz to contemporary music—playing and maintaining a solid beat continues to be my foundation for playing with excellence. This is one thing that's never changed.

The music industry of the twenty-first century is constantly changing and unpredictable. Large and small entities within it must deal with multiple complex problems and obstacles that appear quickly and demand creative solutions. The solution for overcoming twenty-first century obstacles is understanding that the problems we're facing today will have a different solution tomorrow.

The solutions we used to solve problems in the twentieth century have become obsolete, and many in my generation are struggling to adapt to the new climate. If this new generation of musician does not learn to adapt to the fast paced and less predictable industry of today, I foresee a creative stall as they begin to age. I wrote this book to give the current generation of drummers the skills necessary to evolve and create in a way that honors the past and builds the music of the future.

As musicians, we are plagued by ego, pre-conceived notions, stress and fatigue from touring or travel, certain complex highly cognitive musical situations, and stress from navigating the business aspect of what we do. That is a lot for one person in any profession. I owe my thirty-plus-year career to what I will reveal in this book. At its core, this is a system

Preface

of tools, concepts, and checklists that have allowed me to have a solid foundation for musical expression.

The Solid Beat Concept is a checklist of four things that, if you adhere to honestly, will help you convey a musical and solid beat. I would like to stress that these tools are the starting point for a great foundation and not a soup to nuts method.

At the highest levels of complex, intense music we tend to think that the artist must be in tune with some secret, natural element that is communicating through them. For people who feel that way and are hoping to crack the code, this book contains no secret information. There is only a system of questions and a philosophy that has helped sustain my career for over thirty years.

There is no magic box and there is nothing you can physically buy that will, by itself with no effort on you part, get you to your goal. Tools are aids in the completion of work. You still have to physically pick up the tool and use it to perform real work and real practice. I hope this book will help you to discover something about yourself and demystify the learning and mastery process, as well as shed some light on areas of your playing that you may have overlooked or not considered but that are vital to playing a solid beat. The beauty of playing the drums is that we learn to play the basic, simple beat very quickly. But it takes a lifetime to master. The be-ready-don't-hesitate way is the only way. If you have that kind of mindset and are willing to do the work, this book is for you.

The core and starting point for all I teach is—and must be—a solid beat, a groove rooted in a genuine, humble gratitude for the music and those the music serves.

Practice, practice, practice.

Billy Kilson

Introduction

"The beautiful thing about learning is that
nobody can take it away from you."

B.B. King

Alan Dawson's Rudimental Ritual

Besides going to Berklee College of Music, studying with Alan Dawson was by far the best career choice I ever made. Tony Williams was one of my biggest influencers, and when I heard that Tony studied with Alan, it was a no-brainer. Not only was Mr. Dawson the greatest drummer I have ever seen or heard, he was as brilliant at executing rhythms played on the drum set as he was great at inspiring his students. The greatness of Alan Dawson made me not just want to be a better drummer; it made me want to be a better musician. Alan unlocked the door to drumming and its musical philosophy. He constantly challenged and stimulated my mind regarding how to simultaneously react physically and cerebrally on the drum set. It was an experience I had never encountered. He stressed playing the **rudiments** while having good timing: playing a good, solid beat was of the utmost importance. This is the philosophy I carry with me on and off the bandstand.

It would take me decades to realize the true nature of what he was teaching me. I will be forever grateful. Alan's concept was to teach his students to be adaptable musicians. Many times, those lessons embarrassed me and exposed one skill I'm still terrible at. Singing! However, Alan was teaching me to improve my musical awareness.

His approach had two parts: 1) perform exercises within a musical context to build technical facility, and 2) create musical awareness and cultivate maturity.

Everything Alan taught his students had musical purpose and application. When he gave us an exercise from George Lawrence Stone's *Stick Control* to complete, it had to be played and sung to music. When we worked on stick control coordination exercises, Alan would always have us sing the musical form of an AABA, ABAC, modal melody, or blues tune over the exercise.

This training was and is invaluable. He was teaching us to take something non-musical and apply it directly to music. We were learning to become musicians not just drummers. Everything drummers practice should have direct musical application or should include a musical element. Alan's ethos was to teach his students to become students of music and master their ability to play whatever they could think of and be completely aware of their musical surroundings. At the same time, he was exposing our weaknesses both technically and mentally to get us to see and focus on them.

Here's the genius of Alan. Like most beginning drummers, we played **paradiddles** faster than other rudiments. Because it's easy to rely on our strengths to carry the weight of our weaknesses, he would have us learn a new rudiment at a slower pace. He was cognizant of the fact that it's easier to play a paradiddle much faster than a double drag. His teaching method was to have us play our strongest rudiment at the same pace as our weakest. After a few lessons, I noticed that my weaker rudiments were catching up with the ones I executed with the most skill. Building on this skill set helped my drumming and has sustained my career.

Yes, there were moments when I questioned if I should be studying drums like that. I would ask myself, "Am I better today than I was yesterday?" This became my mantra as I practiced on my pad during lunch breaks at work.

Some of the most humbling experiences I have faced were watching my peers' careers skyrocket while I struggled. Some students younger than me were getting high-profile gigs while I worked at a phone company and took other jobs just to make a living. In the end, I did not focus on my peers but rather on my personal learning journey. As I look to the future, I am more excited than ever.

I have Alan to thank for teaching and training me to be diverse as well as adaptable.

I will never forget the time he grabbed my left hand after I'd played a drum solo and asked, "How can you play like that?" I was shocked that I could surprise him. Later we talked about it, and I asked what he meant by that question. He said, "It's difficult to articulate some rudiments with that weird thing going on with your left hand." What came out of his mouth next was even more shocking. "I could fix that, but I'm going to leave it alone. That's going to become a part of your voice." It still amazes me he had a vision for that. While it is at times hard to describe, no doubt he still speaks to me and inspires my performances.

Diversity and Adaptability

For me, the **diversity** and **adaptability** Alan Dawson taught means being able to play many styles of music while having the ability to switch quickly and smoothly within any given period or piece of music or concert, and negotiate styles and choices of music with little effort. The path to diversity requires us to never close doors or reject thinking, because all information is useful in some way.

There have been quite a few musicians who've inspired me to become a drummer who's diverse and adaptable. Whether it's traditional jazz or contemporary music, it's the drummer who maintains a groove/beat throughout their drum solo who makes me take notice.

For me there are four drummers who come to mind. The master of them all was Papa Jo Jones—Mr. Jonathan David Samuel Jones. All modern-day drumming is deeply and firmly rooted in his contribution. Next is Big Sid, who showed his diversity by shaping a drum solo over a beat. Masterful. And Buddy Rich's virtuosic, entertaining drumming demonstrated his mastery of rudimental execution. Yet for me, Sonny Payne with a hint of Papa Jo's taste and Buddy's technique capped with his rock-the-house entertaining skills has yet to be matched. Combine that with how hard he swung the band! That's what I'm talking about. Payne mastered the jazz *feel*, perfectly matching his **groove pulse rhythms** (more on this later) with the band while balancing entertainment and musical integrity. Priceless!

The lesson to be learned from the entertaining ol'skool drummers is to be constantly aware of the entertainment value you bring. The masters focus on ideas that, first and foremost, make a musical contribution, and second, entertain.

Creative Learning

I learn just as much from the masters of jazz as I do from listening to many of the heavy metal bands of today. There is something to be learned from everyone. Creativity can be defined as ideas that have value. As long as you see value in an idea, there is learning to be had. No one can understand more than I the entertainment value an excellent display can give the audience, yet my focus has always been to work on ideas that make a musical contribution to the band. Take the last DVD I recorded as an example. *Chris Botti Live in Boston* is not with the Count Basie Orchestra nor a big band for that matter. However, you can hear my attempt to display the attributes of those things on this modern-day recording. I used an ol'skool concept and flipped it.

For the information to be fit for use, the creative learning must have value and be useful in a musical context that satisfies you and your employer or band leader. Don't worry if you don't see it right away. Some ideas take time to grow and develop. Playing an entertaining drum solo is one of the biggest ideas that takes time to grow. (I will address this more in my upcoming book on the concept of soloing.) A form of diversity is balancing entertainment while maintaining musical integrity.

I can't stress enough that the path to diversity requires us to never close doors or reject a way of thinking, because all information is useful in some way. Creative learning starts with a question: What should I learn?

My answer is simple; learn to play a solid beat in all musical situations. While the answer is simple, it is not easy. Training yourself to adapt requires that you understand the essence of drumming. You must have good time, good feel, and musical ability. The stronger the foundation of core principles the easier it is to adapt to new situations and environments.

Approach all music with an attitude of honest and appreciative inquiry. Learn the history. Take time to learn about what you do not know. Constantly improve your skills and be honest with yourself about your abilities. For example, how are your music reading skills?

We've all at some time in our careers wished that we could be the next seventeen-year-old superstar prodigy like Tony Williams. Tony could handle the responsibilities and had the maturity and emotional intelligence to complete the tasks. That's not always the case.

There is no one big break. You will find that you will have hundreds of little breaks that will lead to wherever you find yourself in your career. Besides studying with Alan Dawson at such a young age, Tony did a few gigs (little breaks) before playing with Miles Davis.

If you come across something you see as a career-limiting failure, don't let that be the nail in the coffin. If you learn to view failure as feedback, you will always bounce back. Failure and experience are the best teachers. A great learning environment provides opportunities for the student to learn, fail, succeed, win, lose, and—above all—grow. If you are not failing at times, you are missing out on valuable learning opportunities. Learn to view failure as feedback. Creative learning helps us by focusing our attention on all aspects of musicianship: the good and those we may perceive at the time as negative.

Creative learning means asking ourselves questions such as:

What deficiencies did the failure expose?
What did I learn from the failure?
How can I use what I learned from the failure to improve?

Competition

It's easy to question our abilities and growth and sometimes be jealous of the success of others, which may tempt us to adopt a competitive attitude toward our peers. But the only person you should compete with is yourself. The greatest thing I can say about that is, someone else's success is not your failure. Are you better than you were yesterday? Are you trying to achieve too much too quickly?

Slow, consistent growth should be your goal, not measuring how you stack up against your peers. Every music student wants to be young and talented. In truth, rarely are young, talented people able to handle what they consider "the big time." I have watched many talented individuals get thrust into situations they were not prepared for. Usually these people get fired and cannot cope with the fallout that happens from getting knocked out of such a high-profile position.

My hope for this book is that it allows you, the student, to take high-level concepts and turn them into practical steps you can use in everyday playing situations. There are no shortcuts and for good reason. The destination is not the goal but the learning you get from the journey.

I hope you're prepared to welcome mistakes as learning opportunities and move beyond them. Now let's look at the tools you'll need to start your journey.

Chapter 1

The Solid Beat Checklist

> "You may be disappointed if you fail,
> but you are doomed if you DON'T TRY."
>
> Beverly Sills

People often tell me that a checklist is not a tool like a hammer. To them I say, you're right. However, a checklist is a tool to help you remember what you might forget in a stressful situation. Levels of cognitive (memory) function are often overwhelmed by increasing levels of stimulus and complexity—stress. Many professionals have come to rely on checklists to reduce human error and increase efficiency. There are many lessons and practices that can be applied to the creative and artistic process, but despite the demonstrated benefits of checklists in medicine, critical care, aviation, and many other professions, the integration of checklists into the practice rooms of musicians and on the bandstand has not been widespread.

The Solid Beat Concept is a checklist, a set of tools you can apply in the contexts mentioned above, and we are starting to see the younger generation experiment with this concept. In chapter six, I will share in detail how I used it to help one of my students when he had the opportunity to play with Gloria Estefan.

In performance and clinic formats around the world, I've been fortunate to share my solid beat philosophy. One of the most common criticism or form of resistance to this concept is this: "Billy, this works for you but no way can this work for me." The way this will work for you is to focus on the music you like, the drummers you like, and use them as references. What has worked for me is constantly referring back to the music and drummers I like. Apply The Solid Beat Concept through the prism of your favorite music and musicians (drummers and maybe even bass players), and I guarantee you will execute a beat with great time and a solid groove.

But before you can do that, it's important to consider your environment and overcome any immediate challenges and distractions.

Chapter 1

Your Playing Environment

How comfortable are you in any giving setting? Is anything in the environment limiting your ability to hear yourself and those around you? Stadium situations with poor monitor setups inhibit a musician's ability to take in information and, therefore, affect their ability to react.

The environment refers to outside factors that affect you and your ability to play. Are you too hot or too cold? Are you playing in an outside venue, a theater, a coffee shop, or a club? Are you playing a drum set provided by the venue or your own?

As musicians, we must adjust our gear selection and personal technique for the environment we're playing in. Some stages and bandstands make it very easy to hear and see while some stages and theaters are extremely difficult to get the sound quality needed to feel comfortable and secure enough to display craft. Your technique must be up to a high level. Only diligent practice and preparation will allow you to overcome these challenges and play with confidence. The best musicians power through these difficult situations with grace and humility.

One situation that comes to mind was a gig I played in a major city. Thousands of people were watching. Unbeknownst to most of the audience, the management had a major problem with several employees. This resulted in a shouting match that almost got the gig cancelled. Cooler heads prevailed, and the musicians on stage, myself included, powered through the difficult situation.

A student of mine was in the audience that night. They noticed the problem and asked me about it right away. I smiled and told them that sometimes stuff like that happens, but the audience and the music are more important than me and my comfort. I have never witnessed a situation where getting into a shouting match or verbally sparring with a sound man or band leader resulted in anything positive.

Before proceeding to the checklist, deal with any outside factors that may affect your ability to play the best you can, and set yourself up for the best chance of being able to hear and concentrate on the things necessary to execute a solid beat.

The Solid Beat Concept Checklist

In its simplest form, the toolset is a series of four questions:

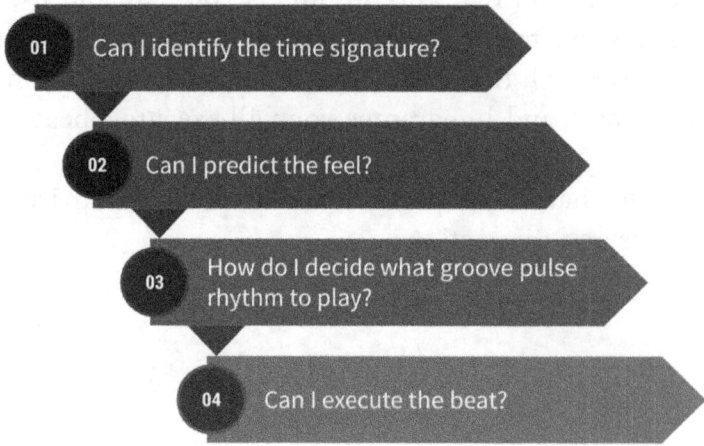

Understanding the questions that drive the decision-making process (whether conscious or unconscious) will help you predict inputs and adapt to new information as it presents itself on the bandstand.

Although not on the list, I cannot stress enough how important rudiments are. Since Alan Dawson introduced me to the Rudimental Ritual, I have exercised it daily without fail. Even when I'm lying sick in a hospital, I need my pad and sticks. It may seem ridiculous to practice the same thing every day for decades, but even after thirty years I still find new ways to develop myself through this exercise. So, I play the Rudimental Ritual every day: sometimes right before a performance. And on my days off, I play it in the morning after my children go to school. This is my time to turn off my brain and become mentally still, focusing on clarity of thought. The only thing that matters is my mental presence and perfectly executing this simple process.

One of the biggest gaps I see between a student's understanding and their execution of a solid beat is their inability to play at different volumes and different speeds. Practicing the Rudimental Ritual daily helps them internalize every aspect of what I cover in this book and what it means to be a drummer.

Developing the Three Senses

To fully realize the benefits of this method you must start training your brain and senses to hear, see, and feel in harmony. Focus on the actual environment you're working in. The goal is to internalize the input from all three senses so it comes together to give your brain the raw information you need to make informed choices. This takes time, practice, and experience. You will start to notice that your senses are becoming more attuned to the solid beat and the musical options available to you as time goes by. If your awareness and the growth of your senses stalls, aggressively focus on developing them.

Hearing

Develop your sense of hearing by listening to the masters. Pick your favorite drummer and five or six recordings of albums they've played on. (See Appendixes A and B for a list of resources.) Listen intently to each and look for learning opportunities, then shift your attention to the rest of the band. Ask yourself these questions: What is the bass player playing? What is the soloist doing? And, how is the drummer responding?

This practice will prepare you for specific musical situations, but to be an excellent drummer, you also need to put yourself in situations and environments that are unpredictable. Jam sessions, one-night gigs, and sight reading all offer opportunities that stress the mind and body. Putting yourself in situations where you're under pressure will help you understand your limits and expose your deficiencies. It may be uncomfortable, but it's a good thing to realize your weaknesses. Being truthful with yourself and focusing on improving your weaker skills will force you to grow.

Your ears are critical to learning, adapting, and executing a solid beat, but they are not the only sense at your disposal.

Sight

A well-rounded, sighted drummer can also use visual cues to improve. Body language is one of the most obvious ways people share information and telegraph intentions. Over the years, I've formed an almost telepathic link with certain bass players. To outsiders, it may appear that we're "in each other's heads." A slight nod or other natural movement can tell me a change is coming. More than indicating *a* change, we're so connected, I can tell *what* change is coming.

Feel

To develop a sense of feel, there is no greater teacher than experience. One of my students spent time working on a cruise ship. After the gig of just six months, his sensitivity had improved dramatically. When I asked how he'd accomplished that, he explained that while on board he played in a jazz trio three nights a week for three sets each night. He played in the ship's steakhouse, which provided an opportunity to play in an environment that was different than what one might expect for a typical gig. He told me he felt that he'd arrived at a new level and now seeks out new ways to challenge himself and improve his skills.

Developing your ability to change the feel you convey with your instrument should become an important part of your practice routine. Learning to adapt to any playing situation is beneficial. I told him whether you learn sensitivity by playing cruise ship gigs, wedding gigs, or—if fortunate enough—by playing with Ahmad Jamal, if you approach it with an open mind, experience is the best teacher.

Listening, watching, and learning to be sensitive to the feel in any given situation helps you adapt and contribute to many different musical styles and in many situations.

Musical Style and Authenticity

To understand what drives musical genre or style, we must look at how we define style in music. The simplest way I know of to define musical style is this: a musical style is a conventional category that identifies certain types of music belonging to a shared tradition or set of agreed-upon conventions.

Style is driven by many things, but the rhythm, mood, and types of instruments associated with each is what makes them recognizable to the listener.

As a drummer, you will come across many styles and be required to work within them. Some of the styles may not reflect your culture, and you may feel as though you aren't qualified to play them. Many students get lost chasing the idea of how to authentically play musical styles they're less familiar with. My students often ask how they should approach this. The first thing that comes to mind is one of many conversations I've had with a close friend of mine who was born and raised in New Orleans and has been through it all—Hurricane Katrina and everything else.

He hipped me to the history of second line, which is arguably the first jazz drum beat and was born from America's first marching band tradition. It originated as a funeral march. First, the musicians would play in a somber fashion, more like a slow jazz ballad, then they would break into an upbeat celebratory type of groove, more party like.

Witnessing this funeral ceremony not only helped me do the obvious, such as thinking, *Oh, that's how that rhythm goes,* more important, it helped me develop an emotional attachment to the rhythms being played. Whenever I play a second line groove now, I experience a transcendence. The feel and emotion flow through the rhythms I play on my drum set.

Blues followed second line and is the root of all modern music. Whether it's Chicago blues, Memphis blues, Mississippi blues, or your blues, understanding its history, why and in what context it is being played, and what purpose the musicians are serving, is the first step in treating the music with respect and understanding how and what to play.

Another homegrown groove is from my hometown, Washington, DC: go-go. Though some would argue it's nowhere as deep as second line, I challenge anyone to find a modern-day funk groove that has not been influenced by it. Go-go music was played to dance to. The purpose was to simply have a good time. Chuck Brown, the godfather of go-go, provided that entertainment for DC. So did DelMarVa. Many other go-go bands followed. Each band's purpose never wavered; it was and still is played solely for the audience to bop that head, pat that foot, or get up and make that body move. Like all musical styles and traditions, it evolves. We have go-go and the styles that came before it to thank for the modern-day hip hop beats.

The popular music of South America, Mexico, the Caribbean, Africa, and Cuba, and the mixing of cultures and musical styles that started 150 years ago, has had a tremendous influence on the styles of music played in the United States. I have always found that students who develop a solid beat and their own tools to navigate all styles of music, whether considered American or otherwise, are able to hear how other musicians play and find musical ways to fit into what they are doing. Music reflects us and is a blend of history, culture, and personal experience. There have been many times in my life when I have been told that because I was not born into a certain tradition, culture, or family I would never be accepted by audiences or musicians playing or listening to certain styles of music. When my students ask how to respond to people with that mentality, I like to quote the great Miles Davis.

> "I don't care if a dude is purple with
> green breath as long as he can swing."

I have been very fortunate to work with musicians that embody that quote. We should all want to work with the best players no matter their age, gender, race, or culture. If you can play well and offer a musical contribution, be a good person, and treat everyone with dignity and respect, that is all that matters. My belief is that whatever works in any given situation is authentic.

Now, let's talk about the basis of your musical contribution, building your solid beat every time and in every situation.

Chapter 1

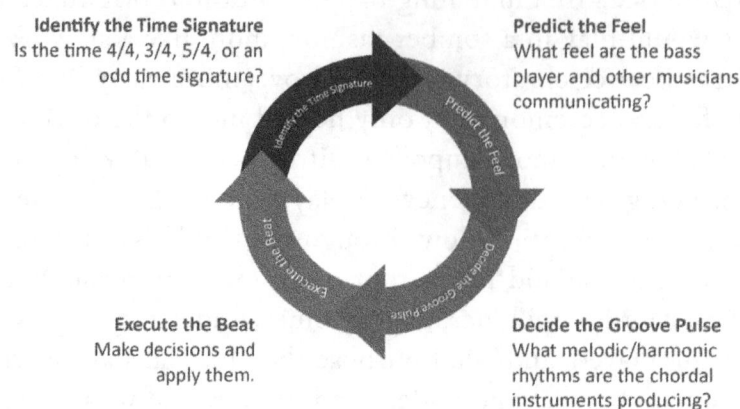

The process of moving through this checklist is finished only when the music stops. I run through this checklist and use these tools many times during each song, subconsciously and consciously evaluating what I'm hearing, seeing, and feeling in real time while making sure the other musicians on stage feel comfortable. The purpose of the checklist is to create and maintain a solid groove that entertains my audience.

Chapter 2

Identify the Time Signature

"I joined bands and made all the mistakes onstage!"

Ringo Starr

Knowing the history of the musical styles you will encounter and being willing to take risks by putting yourself in uncomfortable and unfamiliar situations is one thing. Now it's time to identify the **time signature** of any given piece of music so you can play a solid beat. The bass line, **harmony**, and melody determine the time signature. Usually, the **harmonic phrase** repeats giving you cycles of harmony to follow. When trying to identify the time signature, I listen for the first beat then wait for the harmonic phrase or the **melodic phrase** to reoccur.

Drummers must be able to identify the time signature because often the rest of the band will look to the drummer to establish the groove. That means you will need to be able to "go in cold" and figure it out. As you practice identifying the time signature, don't let the drum line be a crutch. Ignore it because you will be in the place of that drummer when it comes time to play.

The number of beats from the beginning to the end of a phrase determines its time signature. I use information about the time signature along with what I know about the style of music I'm playing to help me determine what I will and will not play. Every choice I make after I identify the time signature is a decision or reaction in real time.

Remember, only the composer has the authority and right to determine how he or she defines the time signature. But musicians are artists and interpreters. Jazz musicians in particular are known for embellishing the music and rhythms they play. In general though, you'll stick with the original time signature. As you mature and as your relationship with the other musicians in the band gets stronger, the music with shift and roll.

You might think of it as a conversation in a group of friends. You may start out talking about one thing, but as the conversation progresses some members of the group may have more input than others and may interject things that might seem off topic to an outsider but that, within the context of the group, flow naturally. Those things might include inside jokes or incomplete references about shared experiences. In the end, the topic comes back around and all the threads weave together. This can only happen when everyone understands what's going on and moves together. So, the time signature provides the framework; the drummer's ability to hear, see, and feel creates situational awareness; and the skill and focus of the group maintains the integrity of the piece of music and vision of the composer while allowing everyone to contribute to something new.

The more complicated the composition, the tighter and more adaptable all the players must be.

In general, drummers stick to the original time signature, but an advanced drummer may—based on the harmonic and melodic rhythms—play whatever time signature she or he chooses. It must be smooth though, and all the players must have an unspoken understanding of and agreement with what's going on.

Before moving on to complicated compositions, learn to identify the time in simple ones.

4/4 Time

Listen to a classic tune such as "Hey Jude" by The Beatles. You will hear the chords change every bar. The melody uses half, quarter, and eighth notes, and the time signature is 4/4. As you listen, pat your foot and clap your hands. This is a straight-forward and somewhat elementary approach, but it works. Understanding 4/4 and how to identify the time signature in simple situations will ground you when complex musical challenges come along.

3/4 Time

The mother of odd time signatures is 3/4. An example of 3/4 time is "Little B's Poem" by Bobby Hutcherson. Like "Hey Jude," the tune's melody is composed of half, quarter, and eighth notes with the chords changing every bar on beat one. The time signature is 3/4, and the style is a jazz waltz. While singing the melody, check out the third bar. It's a dead giveaway. When singing the third measure, pat your foot, clap your hands, and it should become clear that this melody's time signature is 3/4. Again, this is a basic approach but will be useful when tackling more complex tunes. Some **charts** are not as forgiving. The time signature may change within the piece of music. Alan taught his students to master 3/4 time because without mastery of it, creative flow is inhibited when playing the odd time signatures that follow.

5/4 Time

Listen to a standard tune such as "Take Five" by Dave Brubeck. Notice the 3+2 harmonic rhythmic phrasing. Adding this harmonic rhythmic phrase helps the drummer identify this as 5/4. As you did while listening to "Little B's Poem," to identify 3/4 time, pat your foot, clap your hands, and sing the melody. The harmonic phrase reoccurs after the fifth beats. We could count this as a 3/4 - 2/4 melodic/harmonic phrases or as a simple 5/4 phrase. Either way of counting is, in my mind, correct. But remember, the composer is the ultimate authority.

Identifying the Time Signature in Complex Situations

Now that you can consistently identify 4/4, 3/4, and 5/4, listen to what I played with The Dave Holland Quintet on a tune called "Prime Directive." This is a complex situation. The opening bass line could be written as 4/4. The cyclical phrasing of the tune is in six-beat phrases. When this bass line is played, we feel it in six beats. Look at the 4/4 example and compare it to the 6/4 example. It is much easier to read in 4/4, but 6/4 is the natural way we hear it. If you were handed a chart, what would you do here? How would you think about it? There is no one right answer. Any way you interpret the information will have benefits. In this case, each person in the band interpreted the written music based on their personal **Rolodex** of experiences (more on that in chapter 3). Each of us stuck to the melodic rhythms but were free to express ourselves within the parameters of the music. Dave gave us that freedom because he trusted us to operate within the rules of the music and parameters of his vision.

When we understand and master the rules, we can bend them to create a specific effect. Without Alan Dawson's insistence that I practice (and practice perfectly) before he'd let me move on to the next thing, I may not have ever had the opportunity to play something like "Prime Directive" in a situation like that.

Once you're able to identify simple and complex time signatures accurately and consistently, you'll be able to predict the feel.

Chapter 3

Predict the Feel

*"Sometimes you can get too caught up in
trying to think about the coordination.
It's got to be about the feel."*

Steve Jordan

When I talk to students about feel I am talking about making an emotional connection through music or what I am playing on the drums. I am trying to recreate a moment from my past when I felt a deep connection to the music by taking what I connected with and trying to recreate it. Whether I'm playing contemporary or traditional jazz, I apply my effort to creating or re-creating the correct musical feel by attempting to play the appropriate rhythmic phrases with the same emotion I had at the time the music made an impression on me. Sometimes I adhere to the original beat or sprinkle some modern *flava* over it, all while being fully aware of the history of that style. I might be thinking about a funk groove from Tower of Power, but I am not thinking about patterns, specific sticking, or notes that David Garibaldi played. I am thinking about the *feeling* that Tower of Power's music gives me when I listen to it and try to connect the listeners to that emotion using what I am playing. We make hundreds of these decisions based on what we hear, see, and how the audience reacts within a forty-five-minute set of music, and all of them are influenced by what we've heard and felt before and what we've tucked away in our minds for use at the appropriate time.

Creating Your Mental Rolodex

Before the days of smartphones we used to keep important names, phone numbers, and other vital information in a desktop card index called a Rolodex. That idea has never left me. When I think about my personal style or how I approach specific musical situations, I am invariably reaching into my mental Rolodex for information I can apply to them.

Focused research and listening are required to create a mental Rolodex. The goal is not how much you can memorize and recall. The goal is to capture and catalog information in an easy-to-use mental system that creates shortcuts between your brain and body, because it's not enough to know how to play something. You also need to understand why a musician chose to play it. Knowing how an idea works is only the beginning of understanding the limitations of that idea in any given environment. Learning the deep, inner workings while allowing the music to create an emotional imprint and map can help you recognize the limitations of an idea and will make you a better musician.

Research is the process of analyzing musical innovators across all styles and genres. I believe that the environment along with the evolution of the drum set helped the master innovators reach the peak of their creative ingenuity. For example, if stadiums didn't exist, would we have the same level of solo? Would Neil Peart and/or John Bonham have reached the peak of their creative genius where beats are concerned? The same could be asked about the small jazz clubs in New York in the late 1940s and early 50s. Besides the environment, I'm convinced that the equipment that was available to the innovators of the drum set influenced how they played and how they constructed a solid beat during their performances.

The depth of a drummer's understanding of the historical aspects of a particular style should also include knowledge about the types of instruments available at the time. Without both, their growth and adaptability as a musician will be limited. All that information is kept within reach by creating a mental Rolodex. Defining and focusing on the styles of music you enjoy and using the research you've done to develop a mental Rolodex is a critical step for being able to apply The Solid Beat Concept.

Recognizing rhythmic patterns and being able to adapt to them is important, but merely learning a pattern isn't music. Under a brief tutelage by Latin percussionists, I learned that in any genre, the rhythmic pacing of the bass and melody is where the pocket, or groove, is. By focusing on the feel of the music, we serve the audience. Ask yourself what the music is for. What purpose does it serve? Dancing, ceremony, celebration? Mourning? Understanding the music's purpose will help you unlock how to play it with genuine, appreciative inquiry.

Chapter 3

Here is an example of the mental Rolodex I refer to when playing jazz.

The Jazz Feel

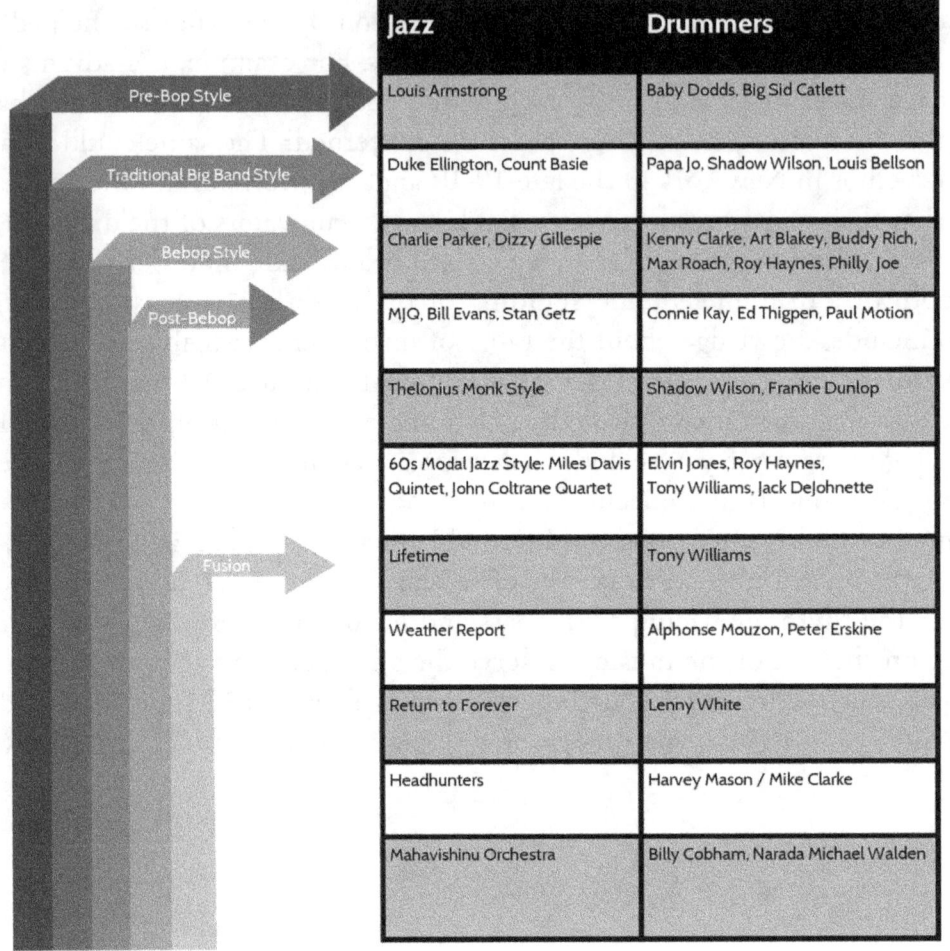

Jazz	Drummers
Louis Armstrong	Baby Dodds, Big Sid Catlett
Duke Ellington, Count Basie	Papa Jo, Shadow Wilson, Louis Bellson
Charlie Parker, Dizzy Gillespie	Kenny Clarke, Art Blakey, Buddy Rich, Max Roach, Roy Haynes, Philly Joe
MJQ, Bill Evans, Stan Getz	Connie Kay, Ed Thigpen, Paul Motion
Thelonius Monk Style	Shadow Wilson, Frankie Dunlop
60s Modal Jazz Style: Miles Davis Quintet, John Coltrane Quartet	Elvin Jones, Roy Haynes, Tony Williams, Jack DeJohnette
Lifetime	Tony Williams
Weather Report	Alphonse Mouzon, Peter Erskine
Return to Forever	Lenny White
Headhunters	Harvey Mason / Mike Clarke
Mahavishinu Orchestra	Billy Cobham, Narada Michael Walden

Arrows labeled: Pre-Bop Style, Traditional Big Band Style, Bebop Style, Post-Bebop, Fusion

Here is an example of the mental Rolodex I refer to when playing contemporary styles of music.

The Contemporary Feel

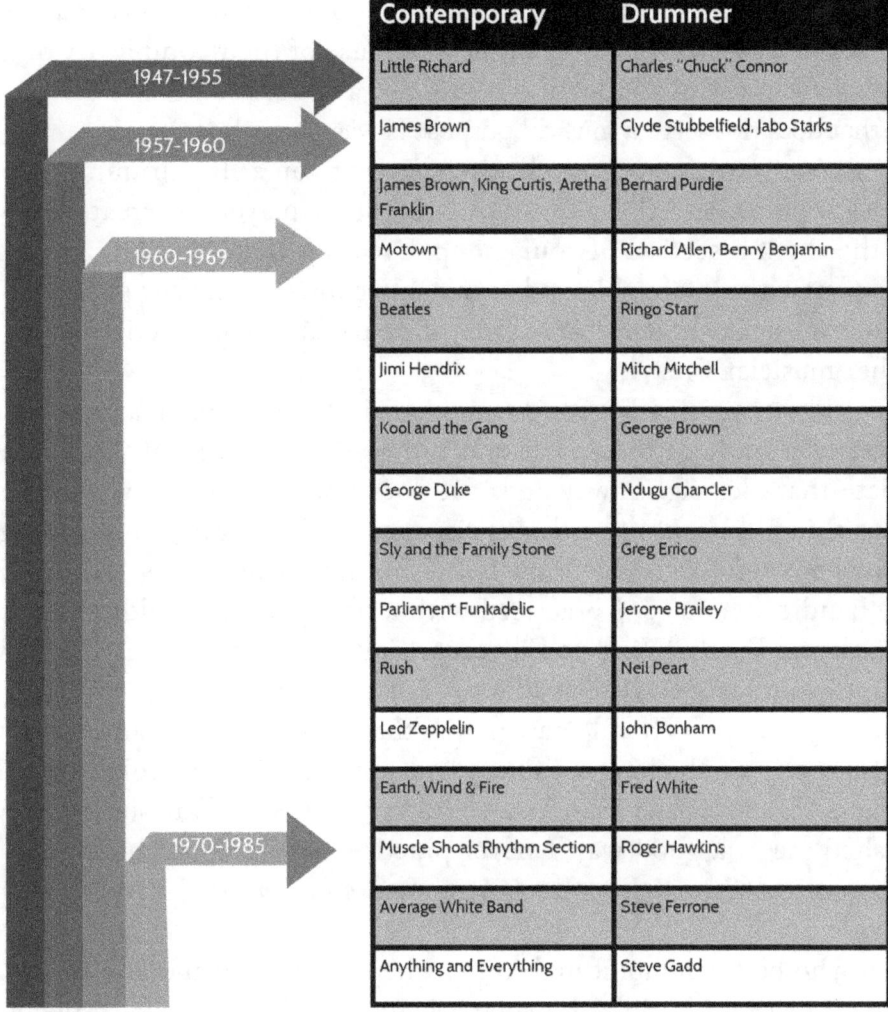

Contemporary	Drummer
Little Richard	Charles "Chuck" Connor
James Brown	Clyde Stubbelfield, Jabo Starks
James Brown, King Curtis, Aretha Franklin	Bernard Purdie
Motown	Richard Allen, Benny Benjamin
Beatles	Ringo Starr
Jimi Hendrix	Mitch Mitchell
Kool and the Gang	George Brown
George Duke	Ndugu Chancler
Sly and the Family Stone	Greg Errico
Parliament Funkadelic	Jerome Brailey
Rush	Neil Peart
Led Zepplelin	John Bonham
Earth, Wind & Fire	Fred White
Muscle Shoals Rhythm Section	Roger Hawkins
Average White Band	Steve Ferrone
Anything and Everything	Steve Gadd

(Timeline arrows: 1947-1955, 1957-1960, 1960-1969, 1970-1985)

Rhythmic Pacing

Band members will never be on exactly the same beat even when playing with consummate professionals. There will be slight variations in the timing of their rhythms (even when there is a click track). These slight rhythmic fluctuations create the pace—or collective groove—of the band. The building blocks of groove and a beat are up beats and down beats. The down beat cannot exist without the up beat and vice versa. Students sometimes focus exclusively on the down beats and forget to devote time to practicing up beats. Young drummers often ask me to tell them how they can learn to play on top of or behind the beat. I tell students to focus on the solid beat and learn to predict the feel.

Chapter 3

When you focus on the feel of a song, you are thinking about the big picture. Focusing on playing on top of or behind the beat without a clear musical picture begs the question "Why?" and does not serve a musical purpose.

Like Alan Dawson did, I encourage students to focus on the musical application of any given exercise or drumming skill. Exercises such as playing with a metronome on top of or behind the beat without a direct musical application do not help you bring a musical vision to life, and exercises that impress other drummers because of their complexity or need acrobatic dexterity, rarely have musical application outside of a drum solo.

Anything that does not serve a musical purpose is waste.

Rhythmic pacing is, plain and simple, the idea that you as the drummer try to match the space between the notes and the intensity of the other players to create unity, a locked-in feeling, with the rhythm section of your group. Creating that locked-in feeling comes from attempting to play with predictable and repeatable consistency. Our goal is not to perfectly match the other musicians but to create rhythmic pacing by predicting a feel that compliments the other musicians' playing.

There is an old saying: Begin with the end in mind. Focus on creating a clear idea of the feel you want, and work hard to execute and bring your vision to life. It's okay if you aren't able to translate that idea right away and if it does not accomplish what you set out to do. The important thing is learning to think, visualize, and execute. Only through experience will you learn what works and what does not. From my earliest days as a drummer, before I played in any band or on stage, I practiced with a bass player. In addition to playing along with my P-Funk and Earth, Wind & Fire records, it was a bass player who I would have to say was my first drum teacher. It feels like yesterday when he said to me, "Billy, match your bass drum with my thumb. When I snap, match that with the snare, and fill in the space and time with eighth notes on the hi-hat." That was back in 1979 when folks were thumbing like crazy on the bass. That was the vibe. You could say that Alan Dawson and my boy playing bass brainwashed me in a good way. I never practiced or thought about beats on top of or behind anything else. I always thought, *If I just hook up with the rhythmic pacing of the bassist, I can't go wrong.*

The person who best communicated to me where he wanted the beat is Mr. 335, guitarist Larry Carlton. He never said, "Billy, this song is behind the beat," or "This song is on top of the beat." With Larry, it was always on-the-job training. As he worked with me early on, I watched his reactions to the music. He would move his body based on where the beat was. He would literally lean backward or forward depending on where he was feeling it. The bass player and I would simultaneously try to hook up with Larry's guitar rhythms and each other's. After a while, I began to hear the way he played each phrase and would lock in to that. When my rhythm was on point, I felt rewarded by his pendulum-like movements. He'd move with a balanced, rhythmic pace: slightly back then slightly forward, almost as if my down beat was the center and the two and four were on the lean. Since my early go-go funk days, and by playing with musicians such as Ahmad Jamal, Dave Holland, and Larry Carlton, I've found that on top of the beat or behind the beat is all about finding the groove within the rhythm section and locking into it.

When I am asked to play a groove, I don't think about patterns. I think about the feeling I want to convey. I flip through my mental Rolodex and think about what I've heard before that gave me that feeling. I think about the emotions I want the listener to connect with. Do you remember a time when you felt something in the music you were listening to? You may have moved your head or body without thinking. You couldn't help but sway or dance to it. Maybe you were getting close to someone while a slow song was playing. Music was the vehicle for those emotional connections and physical reactions.

As a drummer, your job is to contribute to the groove and encourage emotional connections. There is nothing in a pattern that can convey a connection, only a set of movements that will relay information. To make the connection, you must actively engage with all the parts of the band. Listen to the bass, piano, and guitar, and make minor adjustments in your playing to fit into the big picture of what the band as a unit is producing. The music comes first. As long as the band stays together, the musicians within it are reinventing the music and creating as they go. Sometimes it's hard to find a connection and sometimes it's easy, but patterns will not solve your musical problems or answer questions. Exposure and experience are the best teachers.

Having a deep connection and understanding of the space between the notes combined with repeatable consistency are at the core of building a groove.

Contributing to the Music

When the foundation is in place, we as drummers can make other musical contributions. The main questions are: What is available? and What can I play (addressed in chapter 4)? The choices are limited and relatively simple, but making the right ones requires conscious thought.

What is Available?

What is available to you is dependent upon your personal and professional development—your Rolodex—and the tools available to you, namely the drum set. You can think of the components of your drum set as style drivers.

Chapter 3

Drum Set Components

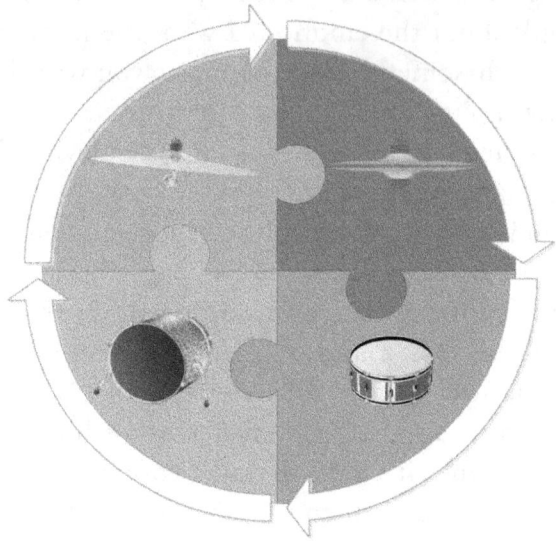

Style Drivers

When it comes to playing different styles of music, I think of the drum set as a family, not just a collection of instruments. Depending on the style of music I'm playing, I value each component of the drum set differently. However, I assign the most value to the component that is to be my main timekeeper, the instrument I'll use to communicate with the band.

For example, when I play funk music, I use the bass drum to communicate with the bass player. The snare drum is there to reinforce the time I lay down with my bass drum. The drum set component I use tells the members of the band this is a funk feel, rock feel, smooth jazz feel, etc. It could also communicate that this is a twelve-measured, blues-rock feel.

With those two components, anyone who hears what I am communicating will quickly understand what style and/or form of music I am playing. The bass player will hear what I am trying to communicate and (hopefully) will find a way to work with and fit into what I am doing. Together we create the foundation for the band. I lay down the rhythmic foundation and support the harmonic foundation the bass player is communicating. The bass player is laying down the harmonic foundation and supporting my rhythmic foundation. Together we create the foundation the music is built on.

If the music is more of a swing-based, triplet style, I will typically use my ride cymbal to communicate the time. I typically use my bass drum to communicate the time when the music is straight-based, eighth-, or sixteenth-note style.

In contemporary, straight-based styles such as funk, rock, pop, and/or Latin, the bass drum is the component I use to communicate the time.

I'm communicating three things to my band mates:

1. Feel: This is a funk feel, rock feel, etc.

2. Phrasing: This is a specific measured phrase or two-bar phrase feel.

3. Time Changes: I'm consistent with my bass (or another component) drum pattern. When the pattern changes, it's because there is a change in the music.

By being consistent and not changing my bass drum pattern every bar, I am creating a stable foundation for the bass player to cooperate with me. In contemporary music, changing the bass drum pattern every bar will cause your bass player to have to work really hard to lock in with you. While there is a time and a place for the drummer to change patterns every bar, it should be musically driven and not because the drummer is not paying attention or wandering around trying to find a pattern that serves their ego not the music.

Contemporary Style Drivers

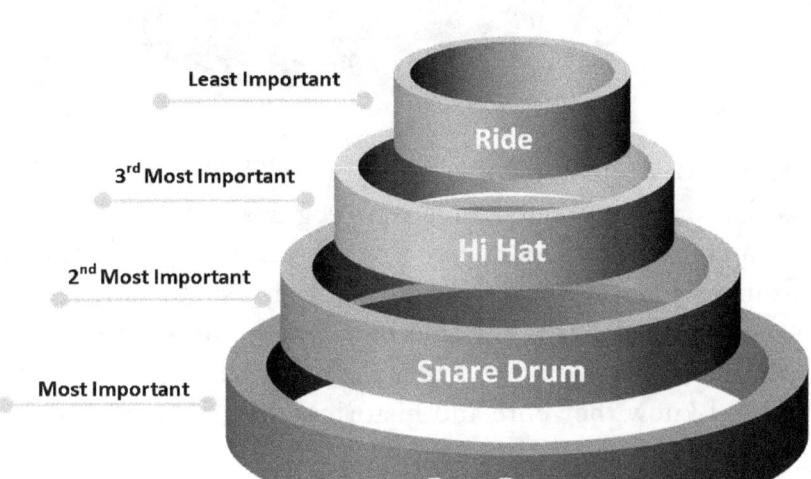

In a jazz setting, I view my ride cymbal as the main instrument to communicate the time and use the hi-hat to reinforce the time. The bass and snare drums are there to support the rhythmic ideas I'm trying to convey. How I play and interpret time on the ride cymbal depends on the feel I'm trying to convey. Each era and style of jazz has different rhythmic pacing and phrasing related to the ride cymbal because style evolves. Innovators such as Jimmy Cobb and Jack DeJohnette are almost polar opposites in how they phrase their ride cymbals. Developing your mental Rolodex by studying and understanding the history of jazz styles and the rhythmic innovations that came out of each era will help you connect authentically.

Chapter 3

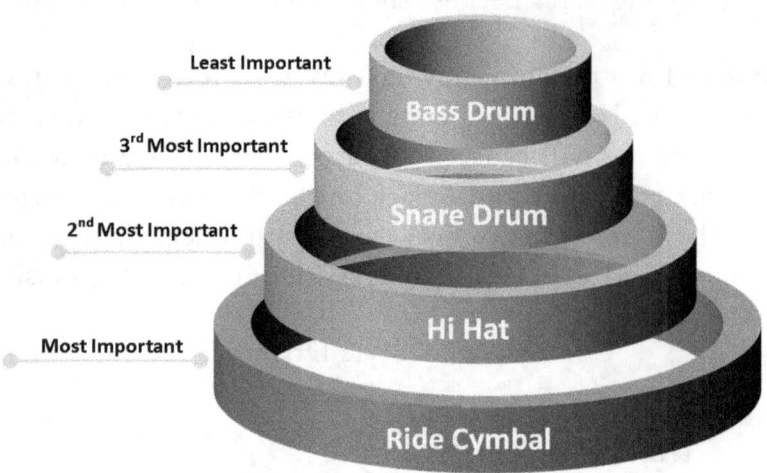

Jazz Style Drivers

Although I keep Count Basie, James Brown, and Jimmy Cobb ride cymbal action close to my heart and go-go at the core of my soul, I am always cognizant that as musical style evolves, the beat and way drummers use drum set components to convey those beats also changes. If you listen to Clyde Stubblefield, JB, Sly, or Funkadelic, they usually don't go more than two bars (measures) without a cymbal crash. Yes, that is where the funk lives, but would you say Notorious B.I.G., Tribe, or DeAngelo aren't funky? When I play a groove, I'm not just conscious of the style I'm in; I know the genre and historical period the groove was created in.

Practice

Expand and contract the beats when using each style driver. Think double time or half time.

Listen to the original innovators of the style of music you're trying to play, not just the current hot band or player, but the original innovators from multiple regions. For example, when studying the history of funk, don't just listen to James Brown. Check out Sly & the Family Stone; Earth, Wind & Fire; The Ohio Players; The Meters; The Isley Brothers; Chic; Prince; Living Color; The Red Hot Chili Peppers; and more. Never limit your knowledge of a style to a single band or person.

Keep in mind that the American drum set is not an exact fit when it comes to other musical traditions and their styles. Experiment. Don't be afraid to apply the drum set where it has never been applied. Who knows, you may just end up inventing something yourself. Remember that all music has something to teach you. Don't close your mind to a style of music just because you don't appreciate it as much as you do other styles, and be open to expanding how you think of each component and its function as a communication device and style driver.

Chapter 4

Groove Pulse Rhythms

"Beyond a certain point, the music isn't mine anymore; it's yours."

Phil Collins

Being a musician is more than reading music and conveying the notes to your audience. As you've seen, it's about conveying emotion, blending past and present, and using the instruments at your disposal to bring about a specific effect. The choices you make about what knowledge and tools to use and not use determine what you contribute to the music.

After determining what is available to you and making choices about which information and tools you should use, you'll need to decide what to play. In addition to—and related to—rhythmic pacing are groove pulse rhythms. This is when the drummer matches the space between the notes and the intensity of the music to create a unity or locked-in feeling with the rhythm section of his or her group. Groove pulse rhythms share common rhythmic phrasing and overlap each other. To me, the groove pulse rhythm is the first rhythm of the bass line, whether it's electric or acoustic. The next groove pulse rhythm is the melody. Once I identify the time and predict the feel, I decide which component of the drum kit I'm going to use to communicate with the band.

Understanding Groove Pulse Rhythms

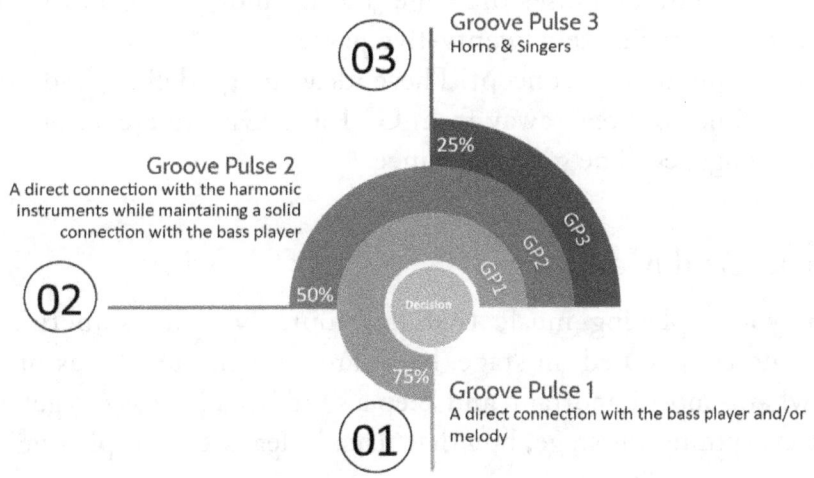

Chapter 4

Groove Pulse 1

Groove Pulse 1 (GP1) refers to the connection between the drums and the bass player or the instrument acting as the bass. In situations where there is no bass, I use the singer as a stand in for the bass and determine my groove pulse rhythm based on their musical input.

GP1 should cover (or interact with) about seventy-five percent of the musical contribution happening on stage at any given time. During your drum solo, play whatever you want; that's your time. But for the rest of the time, GP1 must be locked in with a minimum of seventy-five percent of what's being played by the other musicians. In a contemporary piece of music, your kick and snare pattern must lock in and complement what the bass player is playing because the bass is the foundation of the harmonic aspects of the music.

When there is no bass player, someone on stage will be acting as the harmonic guide post. The piano or keyboard player may be playing left-handed bass notes or **chordal phrasing** that acts as a bass player's grooves. Maybe it's a guitar player scratching funk rhythms while playing a half-muted chord. Look for the musician and instrument that is acting as the harmonic anchor, and take your cues from them.

Groove Pulse 2

GP1 connects the drums to the harmonic and melodic parts of the music. The drummer creates a direct connection to the harmonic instruments with Groove Pulse 2 (GP2).

GP2 should cover fifty percent of what is being played on stage. You might ask how you're supposed to create a connection with seventy-five percent of the music using GP1 and fifty percent with GP2. Generally, the bass and harmonic instruments will play shared rhythms. Your job is to listen to both and merge what the musicians using GP1 and GP2 are playing. If you can find a beat that complements seventy-five percent of GP1 and fifty percent of GP2 while matching the rhythmic pacing, you have a winner.

Groove Pulse 3

Aside from the bass and harmonic and melodic instruments, you can, from time to time, use ideas from the other rhythmic pulses on stage. Horns and/or singers for example. Groove Pulse 3 (GP3) covers approximately twenty-five percent.

Take care when applying this concept. These ideas are guidelines and not hard-and-fast rules. There will be times to break away from GP1 and GP2 to create or release tension so your audience stays engaged. The goal is balance.

Groove Pulses 4, 5, and More

For times when you're playing music that has four, five, and sometimes more groove pulse rhythms being contributed on stage, be aware of them, but focus on GP1 and GP2. Concentrate on what is most important, and keep a solid beat. It's easy to get excited and want to connect with everything on stage, but that usually leads to overplaying, which clobbers everything else that's going on. Sometimes it even gets you fired! Remember that respect for everyone on stage coupled with humility will take you far in this industry.

Making Musical Choices

What to Play

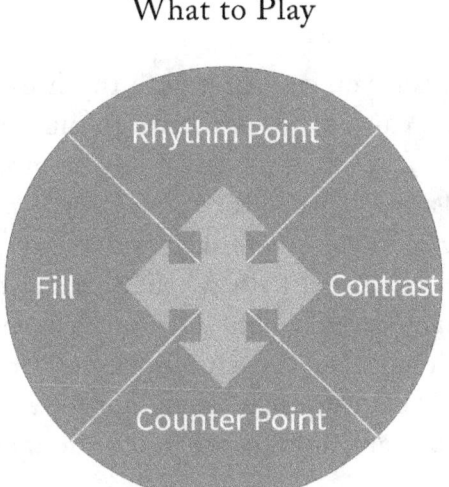

Rhythm Point

When presented with groove pulse rhythms, you have the option of copying those rhythms directly. You might choose to copy a bass line by breaking up the rhythms between the bass drum and snare drum. When you copy an idea, it shows the listener the value of that idea by saying, "This is important so pay attention." But too much repetition can bore listeners. You must strike a balance.

Counter Point

When presented with groove pulse rhythms, you may choose to play a supportive counter rhythm that usually creates tension. Counter point must be treated with care. Audiences have limited attention spans, and music must breathe. If your counter point distracts the audience from the main theme, you will annoy them. Just like in classical music, jazz counter point is when two melodies happen at the same time and against each other.

In counter point, the rhythmic fills of the drummer play opposite the harmonic and melodic rhythms. Counter point is when all three things—drum, harmonic, and melodic rhythms—play under one groove pulse.

Fill and contrast offer the highest level of freedom *in* music. You cannot do this unless you have a clear understanding of the beat and phrasing (groove pulse rhythms), and have earned the trust of fellow players. Playing "free" music does not mean freedom *from* the music or that you are playing outside a musical construct.

In an interview about avant-garde or "free" music, the great Charlie Parker explained it like this: "If you listen close enough, you can find the melody travelling along within the chords, any series of chord structures…It must be built up to. Both the key signature and the chord structure tend to create the melody."

While counter point may—to the untrained ear—sound like a cacophony, somewhere in it there is always a beat or groove.

Fill

When there is space in the music, you can fill it with rhythms, grooves, sounds, and textures. The use of space and restraint can be very effective in musical expression. When managed correctly, space creates tension and large, powerful release moments on stage.

As drummers, we use fills as a vehicle for interaction, improvisation, and composition. But one of the most—if not *the most*—overlooked and underappreciated aspect is **harmonic resolution**. Our beats and/or fills should always support the harmonic resolution of a song. Groove and harmony are what grab and hold a listener's attention and allow them to share consciousness with the musicians and attach emotionally to music. It's one of the most important elements in music. Most drummers spend far too little time developing it however. Developing an appreciation for harmonic resolutions will make a major contribution to your maturity as a drummer.

All the great masters of our instrument were able to develop their unique styles because they were keenly aware of the harmonic freedoms and limitations of the music they were playing. Masters such as Max Roach, Philly Jo Jones, Tony Williams, and Elvin Jones listened to and used harmony to develop their individual styles. You cannot be a well-rounded drummer without an understanding of harmony. Without an in-depth knowledge of it, drummers are missing out on more than half of the important information being delivered to their audience.

When you understand how harmony factors into what you're playing, the importance of choosing a groove pulse rhythm will become clear. And deconstructing the style and motivation behind why certain drummers play what they do will become much easier, because you will become aware of the full picture and won't just focus on the sticking patterns and tricks they played.

Contrast

When drummers ask me about the Dave Holland *Prime Directive* sessions, they are always puzzled when I talk about the shape and chordal innovations as well as the innovative ways the members of the band used re-harmonization techniques to fuel their improvisations. As we played more progressive jazz compositions, the members started to stretch out by using complex chordal substitutions and even more abstract re-harmonization techniques. As long as we were listening to each other, we understood how we could support each other's explorations by focusing on supporting the harmony and harmonic resolutions.

Dave trusted us and understood that my approach was based on listening and that my motivation was to serve the music. Dave knew that my musical improvisation would be from a musical place, so he let me spread my wings as it were. When the soloists were resolving their harmonic choices, or choosing an even more abstract exploration, the group was there to kick things into an even higher gear or downshift to an emotional resolution. Everyone trusted each other and felt supported. I am very proud of the work I did with The Dave Holland Quintet. Even in a situation with so many alpha dogs, we accomplished great things because we respected and listened and responded to each other and put the music first. When all five guys became one unit, there was magic. When you're humble, incredible things can happen.

The common denominators among the masters and drum innovators are good time, good feel, and great groove pulse rhythms, which gives them the ability to execute the most lethal solid beat. Contrasts in pacing, if used correctly and with great care, will give your musical expression shape and clarity.

Chapter 5

Execute the Beat

"It's a great thing about being a musician;
you don't stop until the day you die, you can improve. So it's a wonderful thing to do."

Marcus Miller

When approaching the drums, first and foremost, I want to make sure my time is rock solid. Whether I'm entertaining in a relaxed atmosphere like the one at Fat-Kat's in Houston, or in the studio with the legendary Yo-Yo Ma, no matter what style or setting, my focus remains the same. If I'm not predicting the right feel and applying the right groove pulse rhythms, I cannot execute a solid beat. If I'm entertaining or laying down tracks in a studio environment, I always approach the music with a high level of integrity and encourage my students to do the same. Remember, playing a good solid beat is the key to being an excellent drummer.

Changes in the music are your clues to start the four-question checklist over again.

1. Can I identify the time signature?
2. Can I predict the feel?
3. How do I decide what groove pulse rhythm to play?
4. Can I execute the beat?

It's useful to ask yourself these questions as well:

1. Am I supporting the other band members and honoring the music?
2. Am I responding to changes within the music, or am I trying to force a change in it?

The latter should be treated with great care. If you're the type of person on the bandstand who is constantly steamrolling over everyone else and trying to force the band to make changes, chances are you are curbing, smothering, or even worse, suffocating the other musicians on stage. Make sure you are not overplaying. When in doubt leave it out!

As you've probably noticed, The Solid Beat Concept demonstrates how much latitude you have as a drummer. You aren't locked in to anything and can make choices for yourself. But I would like to reiterate that this is a *starting* point. If your employer or music director asks for something different than what you've come up with using this method, you must follow their lead and honor their requests or suggestions. At that point, focus on the feel and not a pattern.

If a director asks me to play something like Elvin Jones, I don't immediately play licks or patterns I've learned over the years. I ask follow-up questions. I ask, "From what record, album, track, or era are you thinking of?" Then I try to recreate the feel and vibe of that record, not the exact patterns or licks from it.

Some students have challenged me on this by asking, "If that's what the music director wants, then shouldn't I play *exactly* what was played on the record?"

My response to this is simple. No. There are some musicians who aren't aware of the details and rudiments of drumming. There are times when I feel that a translator should be there to translate what the bandleader or band member is asking the drummer to play. Describing Elvin or other drummers to us, especially if a non-drummer is trying to do it, can be a bit of a struggle. The thing to remember is that we all have the same goal in any genre or musical setting—a bounced groove. We want everyone to be rhythmically and musically on the same page, right?

We might be aware of the drummer's skills and technical concepts when playing a beat. Keep in mind some, but not all, of us are aware of **block chord voicing** and other harmonic/melodic terminology but lack the in-depth knowledge and understanding an instrumentalist would have. For example, I'm not the type of drummer who will tell a guitarist what effects to use. I will only discuss with them in the most generic terms the vibe and feel I'm going for.

My point is that when a bandleader or other musician asks you to play so-and-so, they are most likely asking you to play *like* that drummer, and the context or album that may be in their mind may not be what jumps immediately into yours. Just as I said earlier, actively listening is the key. Listen for the *meaning* of what is being asked. If it's not clear, ask more questions.

During the peak of the black rock coalition in the early 1990s, I was fortunate enough to play in a power trio. The bandleader of that trio saw me playing with a traditional jazz band at the Mt. Fuji Jazz Festival. When I return to New York, he asked if I would be down with auditioning for his group. Lucky for me, he chose me to perform in his band. During our first rehearsal, I was thinking about the styles of Mitch Mitchell and Tony, but the bandleader said to me, "No, not that vibe. I want more of an Elvin Jones vibe." I said, "Elvin playing a rock groove?!" He said, "Don't get it twisted. I want the rock feel but through the prism of the master Elvin's **rhythmic groove pulse**." I tapped into my mental Rolodex, and, without a translator, we were off and running to some of my proudest moments on stage with a live band. Playing with those musicians allowed me to experience different textures of music and understand how groove pulse rhythms contribute to executing a solid beat.

The important thing to remember here is that no matter how simple or complex the music, a solid groove isn't static. You will go through this process and checklist as the music changes within each song. When new rhythms and other input come into play, you must identify the

Chapter 5

time signature, predict the feel, decide which groove pulse rhythms to play, and execute a solid beat. The other thing you must do is commit to what you are playing. Commit to the groove. Commit to your decisions.

Chapter 6

Real World Application of The Solid Beat Concept

> "The things that come to those that wait may be
> the things left by those that got there first."
>
> Steven Tyler

One of the great perks of studying at Berklee is that the attending student can exercise their understanding and practice their skills by playing with professional musicians. The reason I teach can be seen in the story of one of my students who was asked to perform with a legendary pop artist.

At the end of every private lesson, I ask my students if they have any questions. One day this student said, "I would like to know what you would do, or better still, what would you play?" I asked my student to explain the context of his question and describe the playing situation. With a nervous smile on his face, he said he'd been asked to be one of the students to perform with Gloria Estefan. I was electrified! I asked my student to stop by my office after normal school hours so I could tutor him. Unbeknownst to him, I'd begun to utilize my tools to help him with his approach and to achieve the goal: rock the you know what out of his opportunity. We moved systematically from identifying the time signature to predicting the feel. We decided what the groove pulse rhythms were and then focused on executing the beat.

While listening to her tune "Coming out of the Dark," it was easy to identify the 4/4-time signature. My student and I determined that it had an early 90s pop-rock feel. My general approach when it's a pop-rock feel is to play beats one and three on the bass drum. My snare is reinforcing the time with beats two and four. If you listen to the track, the drums do not play a conventional role. Sometimes on beat three, you either hear the bass drum or a low tom. On the hook/chorus section, I noticed that the guitar, bass, and keys players are playing a newly introduced rhythm. The accentuated rhythms are on beats one and on the up beat of two. This was our clue to not only copy that rhythm but match its rhythmic pacing.

As Gloria Estefan begins to sing, the rhythm of her vocal line is eighth-note oriented. Although the keyboard occasionally plays a sixteenth-noted background line, I told my student I'd choose the best common denominator rhythm. In this case, it would be notes. These eighth notes are played on the hi-hat.

To make out the groove pulse rhythms, we first focused on the melody (her vocals) and then on the keys. Those two elements guided my approach and helped my student concentrate on the rhythms that were being played, and reinforced how important it is to match the pacing. I explained that whenever I am introduced to a new song or new sound texture, I choose the best component of the drum set to complement the sounds (rhythms) being played or, in this case, sung. As I mentioned earlier, the guitar, bass, and keys play a different rhythm in the chorus section than they do during the verse section. The most obvious new rhythm being introduced is the background vocals. Two beats before the chorus section, the hook line is triplets. My student astutely asked, "On which part of the drums do I play those rhythms, or do I just play a beat and ignore these rhythms?" My response was that if it would disturb the groove, in most cases I would let it go by. But in that case, we played them because the rhythms were so pronounced, we couldn't ignore them. I reminded him that whether he chose to play the rhythms on the snare, toms, or cymbals, he must be precise when matching the rhythms played by the other musicians.

We determined what the time signature and feel were and what he was going to play, then we established the groove pulse rhythms and formulated a solid beat. To my student's surprise, the checklist not only helped him achieve the immediate goal, it also helped with a song he had been wrestling with in one of his jazz ensembles. Thanks to a blend of The Solid Beat Concept and his hunger to grow, this student continues to improve his contemporary and traditional jazz drumming skills and excel as a musician.

I should note that this is my general approach when playing a piece of music. "Coming out of the Dark" has a drum part, but it was written and performed over twenty-five years ago. Unless the producer, artist, or musical director instructs me as to what to play, this solid beat method is the technique I will and have used throughout my career. Now I am sharing this technique with my students and am happy to see it working as well for them as it has for me.

Now that you know how to identify the time signature, predict the feel, decide which groove pulse rhythm to play, and execute the beat, you have the tools necessary to be a diverse, adaptable, and authentic drummer.

Appendix A

A Student's Perspective

Troy Dares

In addition to writing the foreword, I asked Billy to allow me to include a list of my favorite albums, ones I feel display Billy's real-world application of this concept and why I believe they do.

The thing I love most about Billy's playing is his authentic and creative diversity. There are only a handful of players who can sound authentic when playing across various genres and styles. Billy has been able to do that with what seems like relative ease. I have chosen to highlight three albums on which Billy has used this approach. These selections are of my choosing. But if you're interested in more of Billy's work, I have included a short, selective discography at the end.

Hank Jones: *Blue Minor: Live at the Blue Note Tokyo*

This DVD and CD set from Japan is textbook jazz and required listening for all my students. Kilson's playing is at all times supportive, creative, and grooving. Listen to how his ride cymbal matches the rhythmic pacing of bass player George Mraz while blending with the masterful Jones on the piano. When it comes to playing solid supportive time, this album is required listening. Equally important are the drum solos Billy executes over the form of the song: Kilson's musicianship really shines.

In tunes like "Blue Minor," Billy supports the head of the tune even when changing from a swing to a rumba feel; the groove and solid beat are never lost. During the piano solo, his understated playing is supportive. He allows the pianist's ideas to come through while swinging hard. During the bass solo, Billy gets out of the way but still plays great, coming up with ideas and a supportive groove using his sticks. Drummers often use brushes during a bass solo because they lack the technical skill to control a ride cymbal with sticks. Billy doesn't have that problem. After the bass solo, Billy plays a solo over the form of the song. If you sing the chords or melody of the tune, you will be able to hear how Billy is phrasing his ideas and then just when you think you have it, Billy starts to play what sounds like outside and over the bar line. Billy is in complete control of the form during his entire solo; listeners forget about what he's doing and then just when they get lost, Billy brings the beat back to the start.

All Kilson's drum solos are like this. Perfect, textbook playing. Really listen for the rhythmic pacing in tunes such as "Wave" where the bossa nova bass lines are perfectly matched by

Appendix A

the drums. "Come Home Baby" has style transitions from light rock to swing and back. Billy plays perfect transition fills that never lose the groove and always tell the time.

Dave Holland: *Prime Directive*

Odd meters, complex musical harmony, musically gifted players? Yes, please! This album is, for me, Billy's finest playing to date. The compositions Holland and band presented combined with the fearless exploration on behalf of the sidemen were some of the most musically inspired compositions of the day. Tunes such as "Jugglers Parade," "Prime Directive," and "Wonders Never Cease" show amazing compositional sophistication, but even more impressive is the harmonic exploration that the soloists used.

The work on *Prime Directive* showcases what can be done when world-class players are matched with excellent compositions. It's a lesson in how to blend musicality and complexity. First and foremost, the groove is always solid and in the pocket no matter what the time signature or harmonic density is. In "Jugglers Parade," Billy takes a solo that never breaks the form. He follows the harmonic structure while playing outside and over the bar line. If you count the bars in the musical form you can hear that Billy is using the structure to inspire his solo. The title track is rock solid groove that never breaks. As you listen, really focus on Dave and Billy's rhythmic pacing. Each match the other giving the track a groove the other musicians really jump on. Listen closely to the groove the bass and drums create through the entire record. Focus on the interaction of the bass and drums during the solos, especially Steve Nelson's solos. You will find that while the groove changes subtlety, the change is purposeful and perfect.

Over the years, I've asked Billy about the recording session for *Prime Directive*, specifically about the subtle rhythmic pacing changes. His response has been that each musician felt and heard the music differently. One member may have heard an idea as ten beats while the other heard it as a slow five beats. Each could not understand how the other felt and interpreted the musical ideas, but they could hear and adjust to each other. As the band played more together, they became comfortable and started to explore the boundaries of the compositions.

Mr. 335: *23*

This album is a great example of Billy's unique ability to take his voice and apply The Solid Beat Concept to a style he does not have a strong background in. This album is a mixture of electric blues with big band style horns, organ shots, and B.B. King-like funk. Billy plays a unique shuffle style that keeps his voice while still paying homage to the innovators of that style.

The *23* album from Mr. 335 opens with a tune called "Friday Night Shuffle," which sets the tone for the entire album—thick grooves, lots of backbeat, horn shots, and great blues. It also opens with the thing drummers love and hate the most, a "blues shuffle." A blues shuffle is in many ways how drummers and band leaders rank other drummers. When the shuffle grooves so does everything else. "Friday Night Shuffle" shows Billy's unique voice on the drums. No one else sounds like this, and drummers should study this track to hear a great drummer drive the band and keep the pocket all at the same time.

The composition uses horn shots, solo set ups, and rhythmic pacing, and features the legendary bassist, Michael Rhodes. What's even more amazing is that there were no big band-style charts for this session. Everything Billy played on this piece, he created by listening and following his Solid Beat Concept. This track was done in two takes, and the first take was used on the album.

Track two, "Pair of Kings," displays some serious funk with a blend of horn shots and is the true definition of tight and greasy.

Track four, "Sapphire Blue," is a slow 12/8 blues tune in which Billy somehow plays loose and tight at the same time. Drummers especially should listen to how Billy engages with and ignites the band and matches the soloist's rhythmic pacing.

"Slightly Dirty" (track six) is well named. It transitions from a dirty funk groove section into a very tight, clean swing section. Pay special attention to the harmonica solo. Billy once again matches the rhythmic pacing of the soloist, and it really makes this track. The change in rhythmic pacing during the harmonica solo is extremely subtle but makes the solo stand out. This entire album is a study in groove, rhythmic pacing, and all the fundamentals of The Solid Beat Concept.

Below is a list of my favorite albums where Billy used his Solid Beat Concept. I also recommend any album or live show where Billy plays with bassists James Genus, Dave Holland, Bob Hurst, or Michael Rhodes. Listening to all these will give you an education in musicianship.

Billy Childs: *Portrait of a Player*

Bob Belden: *Black Dahlia, Strawberry Fields,* and *Tapestry*

Bob James: *Bob James & Kirk Whalum, Casino Lights 99, Joy Ride, Playin' Hooky, Take it from the Top, Urban Flamingo*

Dave Holland/Dave Holland Big Band: *Overtime, What Goes Around, Not for Nothing, Points of View,* and *Prime Directive*

Donald Brown: *At This Point in My Life, Continuum, French Kiss*

Hank Jones: *Blue Minor*

Larry Carlton: *Deep into It, Sapphire Blue*

Lynne Fiddmont: *Lady*

New York Connection: *Crossing the Bridge*

Philip Bailey: *Soul on Jazz*

Robin Eubanks: *Get2It*

Spyro Gyra: *The Deep End*

Steve Wilson: *Soulful Song*

Terumasa Hino-Masabumi Kikuchi Quintet: *Moments-Live at the Blue Note*

Appendix A

The New Sound Quartet: *Summertime*
Tim Hagans: *Animation Imagination, Audible Architecture, Re-Animation Live*
Tsuyoshi Niwa: *At the End of the Day*

Appendix B

Billy's Favorite Drummers and Bass Player Duos

Papa Jo and Walter Page

Buddy and Ray Brown

Shadow Wilson and Slam Stewart; Shadow Wilson and Wilbur Ware

Sam Woodyard and James Woode

Kenny Clarke and Ray Brown; Kenny Clarke and Percy Heath

Art Blakey and Jymie Merritt; Art Blakely and Charles Fambrough

Max Roach and George Morrow

Alan Dawson and Richard Davis

Philly Joe Jones and Paul Chambers

Jimmy Cobb and Paul Chambers

Roy Haynes and Paul Chambers; Roy Haynes and Jimmy Garrison

Elvin Jones and Jimmy Garrison; Elvin Jones and Reggie Workman

Ben Riley and Larry Gales; Ben Riley and Ron Carter

Ed Thigpen and Ray Brown

Tony Williams and Ron Carter; Tony Williams and Tony Newton; Tony Williams and Bob Hurst

Jack DeJohnette and Dave Holland; Jack DeJohnette and Ron Carter

Ringo Starr and Paul McCartney

Billy Cobham and Rick Laird; Billy Cobham and Ron Carter

Narada and Ralphe Armstrong

Lenny White and Stanley Clark; Lenny White and Ron Carter

Alphonse Mouzon and Alphonso Johnson

Harvey Mason and Paul Jackson

Mike Clarke and Paul Jackson

Richard Allen and James Jamerson

Appendix B

Clyde Stubblefield and Bernard Odum
Jabo Starks and Bootsy
Greg Errico and Larry Graham
Buddy Miles and Billy Cox
Mitch Mitchel and Buddy Cox
Bernard Perdie and Chuck Rainey
Jerome Brailey and Bootsy
John Bonham and John Paul Jones
Neil Peart and Geddy Lee
Marvin "Smitty" Smith and Dave Holland
Jeff Watts and Robert Hurst; Jeff Watts and Charnett Moffit
Dennis Chambers and James Genus
Gene Lake and David Dyson
Lars Ulrich and Robert Trujillo; Lars Ulrich and Jason Newsted
Brann Dailor and Bill Kelliher

Programmers and Hip Hop Influences
Easy Mo Bee
Timbaland and Missy Elliot
Dr. Dre and Snoop Dogg
Notorious B.I.G.
The Ummah (Tribe Called Quest, J Dilla, D'Angelo, Raphael, Q-Tip)

Appendix C

The Rudimental Ritual

The Rudiments and Rudimental Ritual are my meditations for training my mind to be calm, focused, and present. I play the Rudimental Ritual every day, sometimes right before a performance. On my days off, I play it in the morning after my children go to school. This is my time to turn off my brain and become mentally still while gaining clarity. The only thing that matters is mental presence and perfect execution of this simple process.

Practice with different tools such as rods, brushes, dowels, mallets, etc. This may seem obvious, but how many drummers actually routinely practice with these alternative tools, especially brushes? Explore the sounds of your instrument, both traditional and unique. Remember, a good drummer must be able to play all the rudiments with brushes.

Never forget what inspired you the very first time the kit asked you to sit down. Play a beat. You just wanted to play a beat. Everything you'll ever do as a drummer, big or small, starts with that.

In the next book, we will dive deeper into the concepts of the psychological game that is being a musician. I will help you unlock the mental blocks that restrict creativity and limit your mental capacity, and I'll help you create the triggers that will put you in a state of being to experience perfect execution. If you feel blocked or have problems finding clarity and presence, stay tuned. In the meantime, practice, practice, practice.

Glossary

adaptability- The ability to switch quickly and smoothly within any given period or piece of music or concert.

block chord voicing- Usually, a block chord is voiced with the melody played at the top of the chord as well as at the root. There are 3–4 harmony notes that are placed within one octave of the top and bottom (melody) notes.

>Example:
>
>If you have an Fmaj 7(9) block chord with a C as the melody note, you would voice the chord as:
>
>A (3rd)
>
>C (5th)
>
>E (7th)
>
>F (The bass player would play F to support this block chord voicing.)
>
>G (9th)

chart- Sheet music.

chordal phrasing- When three or more notes support the melody; see harmonic phrase.

diversity- The idea that a drummer can play in many different settings and within different genres smoothly and without a lot of mental effort.

double drag- One of the twenty-six essential rudiments.

groove pulse rhythm- When the drummer matches the space between the notes and the intensity to create a unity or locked-in feeling with the rhythm section of his or her group.

harmonic phrase- Supporting the melody by implementing two or more notes, whether simultaneously or in a rhythmic contrast to the melodic rhythms.

harmonic resolution- Resolving a short series of chords or the resolving of chord progressions.

Glossary

Example:
Blues progression is:
I (Bb)
IV (Eb)
I (Bb)
V (F)
I (Bb)

harmony- The chordal (or vertical) structure of a musical composition.

melodic phrase- A melodic or musical part and/or episode in a musical composition.

paradiddle- One of the twenty-six essential rudiments.

rudiment(s)- A set of skills developed for drummers to practice. There are twenty-six essential (universal) rudiments a drummer needs to learn and a medley of close to eighty-five advanced rudiments developed by Alan Dawson.

time signature- The meter of a piece of music.

Recommended Resources for Further Reading and Studies

Stick Control by George Lawrence Stone (2013)
   Publisher: George B. Stone (May 5, 2009)
   ISBN-10: 1892764040
   ISBN-13: 978-1892764041

Progressive Steps to Syncopation for the Modern Drummer by Ted Reed
   Publisher: Alfred Music (August 1997)
   ISBN-10: 0882847953
   ISBN-13: 978-0882847955

The Drummer's Complete Vocabulary As Taught by Alan Dawson by John Ramsay
   Publisher: Alfred Music
   ISBN-10: 0769265243
   ISBN-13: 978-0769265247

Berklee Practice Method: Drum Set by Ron Savage & Casey Scheuerell
   Publisher: Alfred Music
   ISBN-10: 0634006525
   ISBN-13: 978-0634006524

Modern Reading Text in 4/4 for All Instruments by Louis Bellson
   Publisher: Alfred Music (March 22, 1985)
   Language: English
   ISBN-10: 0769233775
   ISBN-13: 978-0769233772

BIBLIOGRAPHY

Bird Lives!: The High Life and Hard Times of Charlie (Yardbird) Parker by Ross Russell

Publisher: Da Capo Press (March 22, 1996)
ISBN-10: 0306806797
ISBN-13: 978-0306806797

Charlie Parker interview with John McClellan. 13 June, 1953. Philology Volume 18 (W 848). CD booklet.

Dave Chappelle quote from interview on "Inside the Actors Studio" with interviewer James Lipton

Mile Davis from an interview with Quincy Troupe

Musicians Buy Line. Famous Quotes by Musicians. http://www.musiciansbuyline.com/musicians-quotes.html. Accessed 24 February, 2017.

Ringo Starr Quote from unknown interviewer

Contributors

Motoka Yoshitomi

Illustration Credits
Troy Dares, graphic illustrator
Alton Sunn, photographs

www.ingramcontent.com/pod-product-compliance
Lightning Source LLC
Chambersburg PA
CBHW081356080526
44588CB00016B/2510